INSIDE VB.NET

IDE DRIVEN CODE USING ADO WITH MSPERSIST

Richard Thomas Edwards

CONTENTS

Introduction

The way I see it, you will buy this book for the code

Certainly not for my good looks or my fantastic writing style!

You are here for one reason and one reason only. You are here for the source code.

If you are not, if you're here in search of a feeding trough of cerebral renditions on just how smart I am, and you aren't. Leave now! I'm sure you will find a 300-page book filled with all the technical jargon your heart desires.

For the rest of you, welcome aboard!

What you are about to see

If you have read any of my other books, you know I really don't have long winded introductions. I hope to not disappoint here. However, I do have something to say.

After this chapter, you will be inside one very large and powerful module that you can call from the form on load Event. The idea is and was to separate the necessary parts of the code into a source that is easy to use and call.

The purpose of doing this code this way is to be able to make the routines simple enough that I can take them and use them for literally almost every way possible. So, you're going to see the same routines driving the same IDE Controls in almost the same exact way.

If this offends anyone, my deepest apologies. There is only on way to write these routines, so they correctly render in the VB.Net IDE and that is that.

The Module starts with this:

```
Imports ADO
Module Module1
```

And ends with this:

```
End Module
```

I am are going chapter break at the top of a routine to signal that a new rendering is starting and at the end of it to show you how to use the routine.

Let's get started!

The initialization code

Making the complex, simple

The initialization code needed to create the recordset:

```
Public rs As Recordset
Public ds As System.Data.DataSet
Public dt As System.Data.DataTable
Public dv As System.Data.DataView

Public Sub Open_ADO_Recordset_Using_MSPersist(ByVal xmlFile
As String)


        rs = CreateObject("ADODB.Recordset")
        rs.CursorLocation = 3
        rs.LockType = 3
        rs.Open(xmlFile, "Provider=MSPersist;", , , 256)

End Sub
```

Since this is short and to the point, we'll be doing what is needed to make the call here. You need to know where the Database is located and what table you want to use:

```
Imports ADO
Imports System.Xml
Public Class Form1

    Private Sub Form1_Load(ByVal sender As System.Object, ByVal e As
System.EventArgs) Handles MyBase.Load

    Module1.Open_ADO_Recordset_Using_MSPersist("C:\SchemaProducts.xml")
```

```
    End Sub

End Class
```

Notice that the module has made the rs, ds, dt and dv objects public so that once they are initialized, you can use them anywhere along the way.

Creating the DataSet From ADO

Below is the code logic needed to create the DataSet in various orientations:

```
Public Sub Create_DataSet_using_ADO_Recordset(ByVal Orientation As String)

    ds = New System.Data.DataSet
    dt = New System.Data.DataTable
    ds.Tables.Add(dt)


    Select Case Orientation


      Case "Multi Line Horizontal"

        For x As Integer = 0 To rs.Fields.Count - 1
          ds.Tables(0).Columns.Add(rs.Fields(x).Name)
        Next

        For y As Integer = 0 To rs.RecordCount - 1
          Dim dRow As System.Data.DataRow = ds.Tables(0).NewRow
          For x As Integer = 0 To rs.Fields.Count - 1
            dRow.Item(rs.Fields(x).Name) = rs.Fields(x).Value
          Next
```

```
        ds.Tables(0).Rows.Add(dRow)
        rs.MoveNext()
    Next


Case "Multi Line Vertical"


    ds.Tables(0).Columns.Add("Property Name")
    For y As Integer = 0 To rs.RecordCount - 1
        ds.Tables(0).Columns.Add("Row" & y)
    Next

    For x As Integer = 0 To rs.Fields.Count - 1
        Dim dRow As System.Data.DataRow = ds.Tables(0).NewRow
        dRow("Property Name") = rs.Fields(x).Name
        rs.MoveFirst()
        For y As Integer = 0 To rs.RecordCount - 1
            dRow("Row" & y) = rs.Fields(x).Value
            rs.MoveNext()
        Next
        ds.Tables(0).Rows.Add(dRow)
    Next

Case "Single Line Horizontal"

    For x As Integer = 0 To rs.Fields.Count - 1
        ds.Tables(0).Columns.Add(rs.Fields(x).Name)
    Next

    For y As Integer = 0 To rs.RecordCount - 1
        Dim dRow As System.Data.DataRow = ds.Tables(0).NewRow
        For x As Integer = 0 To rs.Fields.Count - 1
            dRow.Item(rs.Fields(x).Name) = rs.Fields(x).Value
        Next
        ds.Tables(0).Rows.Add(dRow)
        Exit For
    Next
```

```vbnet
Case "Single Line Vertical"

    ds.Tables(0).Columns.Add("Property Name")
    ds.Tables(0).Columns.Add("Property Value")

    For x As Integer = 0 To rs.Fields.Count - 1
        Dim dRow As System.Data.DataRow = ds.Tables(0).NewRow
        dRow.Item("Property Name") = rs.Fields(x).Name
        dRow.Item("Property Value") = rs.Fields(x).Value
        ds.Tables(0).Rows.Add(dRow)
    Next

End Select

End Sub
```

Why use the DataSet

Since ADO doesn't have a .Net DataAdapter like ADO has with the OleDbDataAdapter, we can't just fill a DataSet, DataTable or use the Default View directly, so we build them.

While all three routines designed to create them are remarkable similar. There are unique differences in them.

For example. The DataTable is used by all three routines. But the DataSet can be a collection of tables and the DataView is the DataTable and the DataSet Table collections default view.

To clarify, Dim dv as System.Data.DataView = ds.Tables().DefaultView is the same as, Dim dv as System.Data.DataView = dt.DefaultView

These routines are especially useful with WPF which will be in other books.

How to use it

Module1.Open_ADO_Recordset_Using_MSPersist("C:\SchemaProducts.xml")

Orientation:

Multi Line Horizontal

                Module1.Create_DataSet_using_ADO_Recordset("Multi Line
Horizontal")

Multi Line Vertical

        Module1.**Create_DataSet_using_ADO_Recordset**("Multi Line Vertical")

Single Line Horizontal

        Module1.**Create_DataSet_using_ADO_Recordset**("Single Line Horizontal")

Single Line Vertical

        Module1.**Create_DataSet_using_ADO_Recordset**("Single Line Vertical")

Creating DataTable Code Using ADO

Chapter Subtitle

```vb
Public  Sub  Create_DataTable_using_ADO_Recordset(ByVal  Orientation  As
String)

    dt = New System.Data.DataTable

    Select Case Orientation

        Case "Multi Line Horizontal"

            For x As Integer = 0 To rs.Fields.Count - 1
                dt.Columns.Add(rs.Fields(x).Name)
            Next

            For y As Integer = 0 To rs.RecordCount - 1
                Dim dRow As System.Data.DataRow = dt.NewRow
                For x As Integer = 0 To rs.Fields.Count - 1
```

```vb
            dRow.Item(rs.Fields(x).Name) = rs.Fields(x).Value
        Next
        dt.Rows.Add(dRow)
        rs.MoveNext()
    Next


Case "Multi Line Vertical"


    dt.Columns.Add("Property Name")
    For y As Integer = 0 To rs.RecordCount - 1
        dt.Columns.Add("Row" & y)
    Next

    For x As Integer = 0 To rs.Fields.Count - 1
        Dim dRow As System.Data.DataRow = dt.NewRow
        dRow("Property Name") = rs.Fields(x).Name
        rs.MoveFirst()
        For y As Integer = 0 To rs.RecordCount - 1
            dRow("Row" & y) = rs.Fields(x).Value
            rs.MoveNext()
        Next
        dt.Rows.Add(dRow)
    Next

Case "Single Line Horizontal"

    For x As Integer = 0 To rs.Fields.Count - 1
        dt.Columns.Add(rs.Fields(x).Name)
    Next

    For y As Integer = 0 To rs.RecordCount - 1
        Dim dRow As System.Data.DataRow = dt.NewRow
        For x As Integer = 0 To rs.Fields.Count - 1
            dRow.Item(rs.Fields(x).Name) = rs.Fields(x).Value
        Next
        dt.Rows.Add(dRow)
        Exit For
    Next
```

```vb
        Case "Single Line Vertical"

            dt.Columns.Add("Property Name")
            dt.Columns.Add("Property Value")

            For x As Integer = 0 To rs.Fields.Count - 1
                Dim dRow As System.Data.DataRow = dt.NewRow
                dRow.Item("Property Name") = rs.Fields(x).Name
                dRow.Item("Property Value") = rs.Fields(x).Value
                dt.Rows.Add(dRow)
            Next

    End Select

End Sub
```

Why use the DataTable

While I have already covered the reasons why in the comments on using it with the DataSet, I'll Just say it is the core building block interface between other data collections and databinding on almost every other control in the .Net family of controls.

How to use it:

Module1.**Open_ADO_Recordset_Using_MSPersist**(“C:\SchemaProducts.xml”)

Orientation:

Multi Line Horizontal

      Module1.**Create_DataTable_using_ADO_Recordset**("Multi Line Horizontal")

Multi Line Vertical

      Module1.**Create_DataTable_using_ADO_Recordset**("Multi Line Vertical")

Single Line Horizontal

```
                Module1.Create_DataTable_using_ADO_Recordset("Single Line
Horizontal")


Single Line Vertical

                Module1.Create_DataTable_using_ADO_Recordset("Single Line
Vertical")
```

Creating the DataView code

Below is the code driven by ADO to create a DataView:

Public Sub Create_DataView_using_ADO_Recordset(ByVal Orientation As String)

    dt = New System.Data.DataTable
    dv = dt.DefaultView

    Select Case Orientation

```vbnet
Case "Multi Line Horizontal"

    For x As Integer = 0 To rs.Fields.Count - 1
        dv.Table.Columns.Add(rs.Fields(x).Name)
    Next

    For y As Integer = 0 To rs.RecordCount - 1
        Dim dRow As System.Data.DataRow = dv.Table.NewRow
        For x As Integer = 0 To rs.Fields.Count - 1
            dRow.Item(rs.Fields(x).Name) = rs.Fields(x).Value
        Next
        dv.Table.Rows.Add(dRow)
        rs.MoveNext()
    Next


Case "Multi Line Vertical"


    dv.Table.Columns.Add("Property Name")
    For y As Integer = 0 To rs.RecordCount - 1
        dv.Table.Columns.Add("Row" & y)
    Next

    For x As Integer = 0 To rs.Fields.Count - 1
        Dim dRow As System.Data.DataRow = dv.Table.NewRow
        dRow("Property Name") = rs.Fields(x).Name
        rs.MoveFirst()
        For y As Integer = 0 To rs.RecordCount - 1
            dRow("Row" & y) = rs.Fields(x).Value
            rs.MoveNext()
        Next
        dv.Table.Rows.Add(dRow)
    Next

Case "Single Line Horizontal"

    For x As Integer = 0 To rs.Fields.Count - 1
        dv.Table.Columns.Add(rs.Fields(x).Name)
    Next
```

```vb
        For y As Integer = 0 To rs.RecordCount - 1
            Dim dRow As System.Data.DataRow = dv.Table.NewRow
            For x As Integer = 0 To rs.Fields.Count - 1
                dRow.Item(rs.Fields(x).Name) = rs.Fields(x).Value
            Next
            dv.Table.Rows.Add(dRow)
            Exit For
        Next


    Case "Single Line Vertical"

        dv.Table.Columns.Add("Property Name")
        dv.Table.Columns.Add("Property Value")

        For x As Integer = 0 To rs.Fields.Count - 1
            Dim dRow As System.Data.DataRow = dv.Table.NewRow
            dRow.Item("Property Name") = rs.Fields(x).Name
            dRow.Item("Property Value") = rs.Fields(x).Value
            dv.Table.Rows.Add(dRow)
        Next

    End Select

End Sub
```

Why use the DataView

I think I've run out of reasons why this code is important. Let's just say it has its place in databinding on almost every other control in the .Net family of controls.

How to use it:

```
Module1.Open_ADO_Recordset_Using_MSPersist("C:\SchemaProducts.xml")
```

```
Orientation:
Multi Line Horizontal
```

```
Module1.Create_DataView_using_ADO_Recordset("Multi Line Horizontal")
```

```
Multi Line Vertical
```

```
Module1.Create_DataView_using_ADO_Recordset("Multi Line Vertical")
```

```
Single Line Horizontal
```

```
Module1.Create_DataView_using_ADO_Recordset("Single Line Horizontal")
```

```
Single Line Vertical
```

```
Module1.Create_DataView_using_ADO_Recordset("Single Line Vertical")
```

Binding The DataGridview to a DataSet, DataTable or DataView

```vb
Public Sub Bind_To_DataGridView(ByVal DG As DataGridView, ByVal dType As String)

    Select Case dType

        Case "DataSet"

            DG.DataSource = ds.Tables(0)

        Case "DataTable"

            DG.DataSource = dt

        Case "DataView"

            DG.DataSource = dv

    End Select
```

End Sub

Making the DataGridView DataSource work with the DataSet, DataTable or DataView

The code to make this work

```
Module1.Open_ADO_Recordset_Using_MSPersist("C:\SchemaProducts.xml")

For the DataSet:
Orientation:
Multi Line Horizontal

Module1.Create_DataSet_using_ADO_Recordset("Multi Line Horizontal")

Multi Line Vertical
Module1.Create_DataSet_using_ADO_Recordset("Multi Line Vertical")

Single Line Horizontal
```

Module1.**Create_DataSet_using_ADO_Recordset**("Single Line Horizontal")

Single Line Vertical

Module1.**Create_DataSet_using_ADO_Recordset**("Single Line Vertical")

For the DataTable:

Orientation:

Multi Line Horizontal

Module1.**Create_DataTable_using_ADO_Recordset**("Multi Line Horizontal")

Multi Line Vertical

Module1.**Create_DataTable_using_ADO_Recordset**("Multi Line Vertical")

Single Line Horizontal

Module1.**Create_DataTable_using_ADO_Recordset**("Single Line Horizontal")

Single Line Vertical

Module1.**Create_DataTable_using_ADO_Recordset**("Single Line Vertical")

For the DataView:

Orientation:

Multi Line Horizontal

Module1.**Create_DataView_using_ADO_Recordset**("Multi Line Horizontal")

Multi Line Vertical

Module1.**Create_DataView_using_ADO_Recordset**("Multi Line Vertical")

Single Line Horizontal

Module1.Create_DataView_using_ADO_Recordset("Single Line Horizontal")

Single Line Vertical

Module1.Create_DataView_using_ADO_Recordset("Single Line Vertical")

Now, we call:

For the DataSet:

Bind_To_DataGridView(DataGridView1, DataSet)

For the DataTable:

Bind_To_DataGridView(DataGridView1, DataTable)

For the DataView:

Bind_To_DataGridView(DataGridView1, DataView)

Please Note:

This is the only time when you should call the create DataSet, DataTable, or DataView with anything but "Multi Line Horizontal". The routines aren't designed to enumerate through any other orientation.

Dynamically binding the DataGridView with ADO

Chapter Subtitle

```
Public Sub do_ADO_code_for_dataGridView(ByVal DG As DataGridView, ByVal Orientation As String)


    DG.Rows.Clear()
    DG.Columns.Clear()


    Select Case Orientation


        Case "Multi Line Horizontal"

            For x As Integer = 0 To rs.Fields.Count - 1
```

```
      DG.Columns.Add(rs.Fields(x).Name, rs.Fields(x).Name)
   Next

   For y As Integer = 0 To rs.RecordCount - 1
      DG.Rows.Add()
      For x As Integer = 0 To rs.Fields.Count - 1
         DG.Rows(y).Cells(x).Value = rs.Fields(x).Value
      Next
      rs.MoveNext()
   Next


Case "Multi Line Vertical"


   DG.Columns.Add("Property Name", "Property Name")
   For y As Integer = 0 To rs.RecordCount - 1
      DG.Columns.Add("Row" & y, "Row" & y)
   Next

   For x As Integer = 0 To rs.Fields.Count - 1
      DG.Rows.Add()
      DG.Rows(x).Cells(0).Value = rs.Fields(x).Name
      rs.MoveFirst()
      For y As Integer = 0 To rs.RecordCount - 1
         DG.Rows(x).Cells(y + 1).Value = rs.Fields(x).Value
         rs.MoveNext()
      Next
   Next

Case "Single Line Horizontal"


   For x As Integer = 0 To rs.Fields.Count - 1
      DG.Columns.Add(rs.Fields(x).Name, rs.Fields(x).Name)
   Next

   For y As Integer = 0 To rs.RecordCount - 1
      DG.Rows.Add()
      For x As Integer = 0 To rs.Fields.Count - 1
```

```vb
            DG.Rows(y).Cells(x).Value = rs.Fields(x).Value
        Next
        Exit For
    Next


    Case "Single Line Vertical"


        DG.Columns.Add("Property Name", "Property Name")
        DG.Columns.Add("Property Value", "Property Value")

        For x As Integer = 0 To rs.Fields.Count - 1
            DG.Rows.Add()
            DG.Rows(x).Cells(0).Value = rs.Fields(x).Name
            DG.Rows(x).Cells(1).Value = rs.Fields(x).Value
        Next

    End Select

End Sub
```

Making the DataGridview work using ADO

Okay, so here's the long and short version on how this works.

```
Module1.Open_ADO_Recordset_Using_MSPersist("C:\SchemaProducts.xml")
```

```
Orientation:
```

```
Multi Line Horizontal
```

```
Module1.do_ADO_code_for_dataGridView(DataGridView1, "Multi Line
Horizontal")
```

```
Multi Line Vertical
```

```
Module1.do_ADO_code_for_dataGridView(DataGridView1, "Multi Line Vertical")
```

```
Single Line Horizontal
```

```
Module1.do_ADO_code_for_dataGridView(DataGridView1, "Single Line
Horizontal")
```

```
Single Line Vertical
```

Module1.do_ADO_code_for_dataGridView(DataGridView1, "Single Line Vertical")

Dynamically binding to the Listview
Chapter Subtitle

Public Sub do_ADO_code_for_ListView(ByVal lv As ListView, ByVal Orientation As String)

```
lv.Items.Clear()
lv.Columns.Clear()


Select Case Orientation


    Case "Multi Line Horizontal"

        For x As Integer = 0 To rs.Fields.Count - 1
            lv.Columns.Add(rs.Fields(x).Name)
```

```vbnet
    Next

    Dim li As ListViewItem = Nothing

    For y As Integer = 0 To rs.RecordCount - 1
        For x As Integer = 0 To rs.Fields.Count - 1
            If (x = 0) Then
                li = lv.Items.Add(rs.Fields(x).Value)
            Else
                li.SubItems.Add(rs.Fields(x).Value)
            End If
        Next
        rs.MoveNext()
    Next


Case "Multi Line Vertical"


    lv.Columns.Add("Property Name")
    For y As Integer = 0 To rs.RecordCount - 1
        lv.Columns.Add("Row" & y)
    Next

    Dim li As ListViewItem = Nothing

    For x As Integer = 0 To rs.Fields.Count - 1
        li = lv.Items.Add(rs.Fields(x).Name)
        rs.MoveFirst()
        For y As Integer = 0 To rs.RecordCount - 1
            li.SubItems.Add(rs.Fields(x).Value)
            rs.MoveNext()
        Next
    Next

Case "Single Line Horizontal"

    For x As Integer = 0 To rs.Fields.Count - 1
        lv.Columns.Add(rs.Fields(x).Name)
    Next
```

```vb
Dim li As ListViewItem = Nothing

For y As Integer = 0 To rs.RecordCount - 1
    For x As Integer = 0 To rs.Fields.Count - 1
        If (x = 0) Then
            li = lv.Items.Add(rs.Fields(x).Value)
        Else
            li.SubItems.Add(rs.Fields(x).Value)
        End If
    Next
    Exit For
Next


Case "Single Line Vertical"


    lv.Columns.Add("Property Name")
    lv.Columns.Add("Property Value")

    Dim li As ListViewItem = Nothing

    For x As Integer = 0 To rs.Fields.Count - 1
        li = lv.Items.Add(rs.Fields(x).Name)
        li.SubItems.Add(rs.Fields(x).Value)
    Next

End Select

End Sub
```

Making the Listview work using ADO

This time, we use the following code:

```
Module1.Open_ADO_Recordset_Using_MSPersist("C:\SchemaProducts.xml")
```

Orientation:

Multi Line Horizontal

```
Module1.do_ADO_code_for_ListView(ListView1, "Multi Line Horizontal")
```

Multi Line Vertical

```
Module1.do_ADO_code_for_ListView(ListView1, "Multi Line Vertical")
```

Single Line Horizontal

```
Module1.do_ADO_code_for_ListView(ListView1, "Single Line Horizontal")
```

Single Line Vertical

```
Module1.do_ADO_code_for_ListView(ListView1, "Single Line Vertical")
```

Dynamically binding ADO to the MSFlexgrid

```vb
Public Sub do_ADO_code_for_MSFlexGrid(ByVal fg As
AxMSFlexGridLib.AxMSFlexGrid, ByVal Orientation As String)


    fg.Clear()


    Select Case Orientation


        Case "Multi Line Horizontal"


            fg.Cols = rs.Fields.Count + 1
            fg.Rows = rs.RecordCount + 1
            For x As Integer = 0 To rs.Fields.Count - 1
                fg.set_TextMatrix(0, x + 1, rs.Fields(x).Name)
            Next

            rs.MoveFirst()

            For y As Integer = 0 To rs.RecordCount - 1
                For x As Integer = 0 To rs.Fields.Count - 1
```

```vbnet
            fg.set_TextMatrix(y + 1, x + 1, rs.Fields(x).Value)
        Next
        rs.MoveNext()
    Next


Case "Multi Line Vertical"

    fg.Rows = rs.Fields.Count + 1
    fg.Cols = rs.RecordCount + 1
    For x As Integer = 0 To rs.Fields.Count - 1
        fg.set_TextMatrix(x + 1, 0, rs.Fields(x).Name)
    Next

    For y As Integer = 0 To rs.RecordCount - 1
        For x As Integer = 0 To rs.Fields.Count - 1
            fg.set_TextMatrix(x + 1, y + 1, rs.Fields(x).Value)
        Next
    Next


Case "Single Line Horizontal"

    fg.Cols = rs.Fields.Count + 1
    fg.Rows = 2
    For x As Integer = 0 To rs.Fields.Count - 1
        fg.set_TextMatrix(0, x + 1, rs.Fields(x).Name)
    Next

    For y As Integer = 0 To rs.RecordCount - 1
        For x As Integer = 0 To rs.Fields.Count - 1
            fg.set_TextMatrix(y + 1, x + 1, rs.Fields(x).Value)
        Next
        Exit For
    Next


Case "Single Line Vertical"
```

```
        fg.Rows = rs.Fields.Count + 1
        fg.Cols = 2
        For x As Integer = 0 To rs.Fields.Count - 1
            fg.set_TextMatrix(x + 1, 0, rs.Fields(x).Name)
        Next

        For y As Integer = 0 To rs.RecordCount - 1
            For x As Integer = 0 To rs.Fields.Count - 1
                fg.set_TextMatrix(x + 1, y + 1, rs.Fields(x).Value)
            Next
            Exit For
        Next


    End Select

End Sub
```

Making the MSFlexgrid work using ADO

These routines will get the job done:

Module1.Open_ADO_Recordset_Using_MSPersist("C:\SchemaProducts.xml")

Orientation:

Multi Line Horizontal

Module1.do_ADO_code_for_MSFlexGrid(AxMSFlexGrid1
, "Multi Line Horizontal")

Multi Line Vertical

Module1.do_ADO_code_for_MSFlexGrid(AxMSFlexGrid1
, "Multi Line Vertical")

Single Line Horizontal

Module1.do_ADO_code_for_MSFlexGrid(AxMSFlexGrid1
, "Single Line Horizontal")

Single Line Vertical

Module1.do_ADO_code_for_MSFlexGrid(AxMSFlexGrid1
, "Single Line Vertical")

Dynamically binding ADO to the Spreadsheet

```
Public Sub do_ADO_code_for_Spreadsheet(ByVal sp1 As
AxMicrosoft.Office.Interop.Owc11.AxSpreadsheet, ByVal Orientation As String)


    sp1.ActiveSheet.Cells.Clear()



    Select Case Orientation


        Case "Multi Line Horizontal"



            For x As Integer = 0 To rs.Fields.Count - 1
                sp1.ActiveSheet.Cells(1, x + 1) = rs.Fields(x).Name
            Next

            rs.MoveFirst()

            For y As Integer = 0 To rs.RecordCount - 1
                For x As Integer = 0 To rs.Fields.Count - 1
                    sp1.ActiveSheet.Cells(y + 1, x + 1) = rs.Fields(x).Value
```

```
                Next
                rs.MoveNext()
            Next



Case "Multi Line Vertical"


            For x As Integer = 0 To rs.Fields.Count - 1
                sp1.ActiveSheet.Cells(x + 1, 1) = rs.Fields(x).Name
            Next

            For y As Integer = 0 To rs.RecordCount - 1
                rs.MoveFirst()
                For x As Integer = 0 To rs.Fields.Count - 1
                    sp1.ActiveSheet.Cells(x + 1, y + 2) = rs.Fields(x).Value
                Next
                rs.MoveNext()
            Next



Case "Single Line Horizontal"


            For x As Integer = 0 To rs.Fields.Count - 1
                sp1.ActiveSheet.Cells(1, x + 1) = rs.Fields(x).Name
            Next

            rs.MoveFirst()

            For y As Integer = 0 To rs.RecordCount - 1
                For x As Integer = 0 To rs.Fields.Count - 1
                    sp1.ActiveSheet.Cells(y + 2, x + 1) = rs.Fields(x).Value
                Next
                Exit For
            Next



Case "Single Line Vertical"
```

```vbnet
        For x As Integer = 0 To rs.Fields.Count - 1
            sp1.ActiveSheet.Cells(x + 1, 1) = rs.Fields(x).Name
        Next

        rs.MoveFirst()

        For y As Integer = 0 To rs.RecordCount - 1
            For x As Integer = 0 To rs.Fields.Count - 1
                sp1.ActiveSheet.Cells(x + 1, y + 2) = rs.Fields(x).Value
            Next
            Exit For
        Next


    End Select

End Sub
```

Making the Spreadsheet work using ADO

Routines for the Spreadsheet will get the job done:

```
Module1.Open_ADO_Recordset_Using_MSPersist("C:\SchemaProducts.xml")
```

Orientation:

Multi Line Horizontal

```
Module1.do_ADO_code_for_Spreadsheet(AxSpreadsheet1
, "Multi Line Horizontal")
```

Multi Line Vertical

```
Module1.do_ADO_code_for_Spreadsheet(AxSpreadsheet1
, "Multi Line Vertical")
```

Single Line Horizontal

```
Module1.do_ADO_code_for_Spreadsheet(AxSpreadsheet1
, "Single Line Horizontal")
```

Single Line Vertical

```
Module1.do_ADO_code_for_Spreadsheet(AxSpreadsheet1
, "Single Line Vertical")
```

Working with the DataGridView using A DataSet

```
Public Sub do_DataSet_code_for_dataGridView(ByVal DG As
DataGridView, ByVal Orientation As String)


        DG.Rows.Clear()
        DG.Columns.Clear()


        Select Case Orientation


            Case "Multi Line Horizontal"

                For x As Integer = 0 To
ds.Tables(0).Columns.Count - 1

DG.Columns.Add(ds.Tables(0).Columns(x).Caption,
ds.Tables(0).Columns(x).Caption)
                Next

                For y As Integer = 0 To ds.Tables(0).Rows.Count -
1
                    DG.Rows.Add()
                    For x As Integer = 0 To
ds.Tables(0).Columns.Count - 1
                        DG.Rows(y).Cells(x).Value =
ds.Tables(0).Rows(y).Item(ds.Tables(0).Columns(x).Caption)
                    Next
```

```vb
                    rs.MoveNext()
                Next


            Case "Multi Line Vertical"


                DG.Columns.Add("Property Name", "Property Name")
                For y As Integer = 0 To ds.Tables(0).Rows.Count -
1
                    DG.Columns.Add("Row" & y, "Row" & y)
                Next

                For x As Integer = 0 To
ds.Tables(0).Columns.Count - 1
                    DG.Rows.Add()
                    DG.Rows(x).Cells(0).Value =
ds.Tables(0).Columns(x).Caption
                    For y As Integer = 0 To
ds.Tables(0).Rows.Count - 1
                        DG.Rows(x).Cells(y + 1).Value =
ds.Tables(0).Rows(y).Item(ds.Tables(0).Columns(x).Caption)
                    Next
                Next

            Case "Single Line Horizontal"


                For x As Integer = 0 To
ds.Tables(0).Columns.Count - 1

DG.Columns.Add(ds.Tables(0).Columns(x).Caption,
ds.Tables(0).Columns(x).Caption)
                Next

                For y As Integer = 0 To ds.Tables(0).Rows.Count -
1
                    DG.Rows.Add()
                    For x As Integer = 0 To
ds.Tables(0).Columns.Count - 1
                        DG.Rows(y).Cells(x).Value =
ds.Tables(0).Rows(y).Item(ds.Tables(0).Columns(x).Caption)
                    Next
                    Exit For
                Next
```

```vb
        Case "Single Line Vertical"

                DG.Columns.Add("Property Name", "Property Name")
                DG.Columns.Add("Property Value", "Property
Value")

                For x As Integer = 0 To
ds.Tables(0).Columns.Count - 1
                    DG.Rows.Add()
                    DG.Rows(x).Cells(0).Value =
ds.Tables(0).Columns(x).Caption
                    DG.Rows(x).Cells(1).Value =
ds.Tables(0).Rows(0).Item(ds.Tables(0).Columns(x).Caption)
                Next

        End Select

    End Sub
```

Making the DataGridView work using a DataSet

To make this code work, we piece together three routines:

Module1.Open_ADO_Recordset_Using_MSPersist("C:\SchemaProducts.xml")
Module1.Create_DataSet_using_ADO_Recordset("Multi Line Horizontal")

Now, depending on what view we want to create:

Orientation:

Multi Line Horizontal

Module1.do_DataSet_code_for_DataGridView(DataGridView1, "Multi Line Horizontal")

Multi Line Vertical

Module1.do_DataSet_code_for_ DataGridView(DataGridView1, "Multi Line Vertical")

Single Line Horizontal

Module1.do_DataSet_code_for_ DataGridView(DataGridView1, "Single Line Horizontal")

Single Line Vertical

Module1.do_DataSet_code_for_ DataGridView(DataGridView1, "Single Line Vertical")

Working with the DataGridView using a DataTable

```vbnet
Public Sub do_DataTable_code_for_dataGridView(ByVal DG As
DataGridView, ByVal Orientation As String)


        DG.Rows.Clear()
        DG.Columns.Clear()


        Select Case Orientation


            Case "Multi Line Horizontal"

                For x As Integer = 0 To dt.Columns.Count - 1
                    DG.Columns.Add(dt.Columns(x).Caption,
dt.Columns(x).Caption)
                Next

                For y As Integer = 0 To dt.Rows.Count - 1
                    DG.Rows.Add()
                    For x As Integer = 0 To dt.Columns.Count - 1
                        DG.Rows(y).Cells(x).Value =
dt.Rows(y).Item(dt.Columns(x).Caption)
                    Next
                    rs.MoveNext()
```

```vb
                    Next

            Case "Multi Line Vertical"

                    DG.Columns.Add("Property Name", "Property Name")
                    For y As Integer = 0 To dt.Rows.Count - 1
                        DG.Columns.Add("Row" & y, "Row" & y)
                    Next

                    For x As Integer = 0 To dt.Columns.Count - 1
                        DG.Rows.Add()
                        DG.Rows(x).Cells(0).Value =
dt.Columns(x).Caption
                            For y As Integer = 0 To dt.Rows.Count - 1
                                DG.Rows(x).Cells(y + 1).Value =
dt.Rows(y).Item(dt.Columns(x).Caption)
                            Next
                    Next

            Case "Single Line Horizontal"

                    For x As Integer = 0 To dt.Columns.Count - 1
                        DG.Columns.Add(dt.Columns(x).Caption,
dt.Columns(x).Caption)
                    Next

                    For y As Integer = 0 To dt.Rows.Count - 1
                        DG.Rows.Add()
                        For x As Integer = 0 To dt.Columns.Count - 1
                            DG.Rows(y).Cells(x).Value =
dt.Rows(y).Item(dt.Columns(x).Caption)
                        Next
                        Exit For
                    Next

            Case "Single Line Vertical"

                    DG.Columns.Add("Property Name", "Property Name")
                    DG.Columns.Add("Property Value", "Property
Value")
```

```vbnet
            For x As Integer = 0 To dt.Columns.Count - 1
                DG.Rows.Add()
                DG.Rows(x).Cells(0).Value =
dt.Columns(x).Caption
                DG.Rows(x).Cells(1).Value =
dt.Rows(0).Item(dt.Columns(x).Caption)
            Next

        End Select

    End Sub
```

Making the DataGridView work using a DataTable

To make this code work, we piece together three routines:

Module1.Open_ADO_Recordset_Using_MSPersist("C:\SchemaProducts.xml")

Module1.Create_DataTable_using_ADO_Recordset("Multi Line Horizontal")

Now, depending on what view we want to create:

Orientation:

Multi Line Horizontal

Module1.do_DataTable_code_for_DataGridView(DataGridView1, "Multi Line Horizontal")

Multi Line Vertical

Module1.do_DataTable_code_for_ DataGridView(DataGridView1, "Multi Line Vertical")

Single Line Horizontal

Module1.do_DataTable_code_for_ DataGridView(DataGridView1, "Single Line Horizontal")

Single Line Vertical

Module1.do_DataTable_code_for_ DataGridView(DataGridView1, "Single Line Vertical")

Working with the DataGridView using A DataView

```vbnet
Public Sub do_DataView_code_for_dataGridView(ByVal DG As
DataGridView, ByVal Orientation As String)


        DG.Rows.Clear()
        DG.Columns.Clear()


        Select Case Orientation


            Case "Multi Line Horizontal"

                For x As Integer = 0 To dv.Table.Columns.Count -
1
                    DG.Columns.Add(dv.Table.Columns(x).Caption,
dv.Table.Columns(x).Caption)
                Next

                For y As Integer = 0 To dv.Table.Rows.Count - 1
                    DG.Rows.Add()
                    For x As Integer = 0 To
dv.Table.Columns.Count - 1
```

```
                        DG.Rows(y).Cells(x).Value =
dv.Table.Rows(y).Item(dv.Table.Columns(x).Caption)
                Next
                rs.MoveNext()
        Next


    Case "Multi Line Vertical"


            DG.Columns.Add("Property Name", "Property Name")
            For y As Integer = 0 To dv.Table.Rows.Count - 1
                DG.Columns.Add("Row" & y, "Row" & y)
            Next

            For x As Integer = 0 To dv.Table.Columns.Count -
1
                DG.Rows.Add()
                DG.Rows(x).Cells(0).Value =
dv.Table.Columns(x).Caption
                For y As Integer = 0 To dv.Table.Rows.Count -
1
                    DG.Rows(x).Cells(y + 1).Value =
dv.Table.Rows(y).Item(dv.Table.Columns(x).Caption)
                Next
            Next

    Case "Single Line Horizontal"


            For x As Integer = 0 To dv.Table.Columns.Count -
1
                DG.Columns.Add(dv.Table.Columns(x).Caption,
dv.Table.Columns(x).Caption)
            Next

            For y As Integer = 0 To dv.Table.Rows.Count - 1
                DG.Rows.Add()
                For x As Integer = 0 To
dv.Table.Columns.Count - 1
                    DG.Rows(y).Cells(x).Value =
dv.Table.Rows(y).Item(dv.Table.Columns(x).Caption)
                Next
                Exit For
            Next
```

```vbnet
            Case "Single Line Vertical"

                DG.Columns.Add("Property Name", "Property Name")
                DG.Columns.Add("Property Value", "Property
Value")

                For x As Integer = 0 To dv.Table.Columns.Count -
1
                    DG.Rows.Add()
                    DG.Rows(x).Cells(0).Value =
dv.Table.Columns(x).Caption
                    DG.Rows(x).Cells(1).Value =
dv.Table.Rows(0).Item(dv.Table.Columns(x).Caption)
                Next

        End Select

    End Sub
```

Making the DataGridView work using a DataView

To make this code work, we piece together three routines:

Module1.Open_ADO_Recordset_Using_MSPersist("C:\SchemaProducts.xml")
Module1.Create_DataView_using_ADO_Recordset("Multi Line Horizontal")

Now, depending on what view we want to create:

Orientation:

Multi Line Horizontal

Module1.do_DataView_code_for_DataGridView(DataGridView1, "Multi Line Horizontal")

Multi Line Vertical

Module1.do_DataView_code_for_ DataGridView(DataGridView1, "Multi Line Vertical")

Single Line Horizontal

Module1.do_DataView_code_for_ DataGridView(DataGridView1, "Single Line Horizontal")

Single Line Vertical

Module1.do_DataView_code_for_ DataGridView(DataGridView1, "Single Line Vertical")

Working with the Listview using a DataSet

Chapter Subtitle

```
Public Sub do_DataSet_code_for_ListView(ByVal lv As ListView, ByVal
Orientation As String)


    lv.Items.Clear()
    lv.Columns.Clear()


    Select Case Orientation


        Case "Multi Line Horizontal"

            For x As Integer = 0 To ds.Tables(0).Columns.Count - 1
                lv.Columns.Add(ds.Tables(0).Columns(x).Caption)
            Next

            Dim li As ListViewItem = Nothing

            For y As Integer = 0 To ds.Tables(0).Rows.Count - 1
```

```vbnet
                    For x As Integer = 0 To ds.Tables(0).Columns.Count - 1
                        If (x = 0) Then
                            li                                                    =
lv.Items.Add(ds.Tables(0).Rows(y).Item(ds.Tables(0).Columns(x)))
                        Else

li.SubItems.Add(ds.Tables(0).Rows(y).Item(ds.Tables(0).Columns(x)))
                        End If
                    Next
                Next


            Case "Multi Line Vertical"


                lv.Columns.Add("Property Name")
                For y As Integer = 0 To ds.Tables(0).Rows.Count - 1
                    lv.Columns.Add("Row" & y)
                Next

                Dim li As ListViewItem = Nothing

                For x As Integer = 0 To ds.Tables(0).Columns.Count - 1
                    li = lv.Items.Add(ds.Tables(0).Columns(x).Caption)
                    For y As Integer = 0 To ds.Tables(0).Rows.Count - 1

li.SubItems.Add(ds.Tables(0).Rows(y).Item(ds.Tables(0).Columns(x).Caption))
                    Next
                Next

            Case "Single Line Horizontal"


                For x As Integer = 0 To ds.Tables(0).Columns.Count - 1
                    lv.Columns.Add(ds.Tables(0).Columns(x).Caption)
                Next

                Dim li As ListViewItem = Nothing

                For y As Integer = 0 To ds.Tables(0).Rows.Count - 1
```

```vbnet
                    For x As Integer = 0 To ds.Tables(0).Columns.Count - 1
                        If (x = 0) Then
                            li                                                      =
lv.Items.Add(ds.Tables(0).Rows(y).Item(ds.Tables(0).Columns(x).Caption))
                        Else

li.SubItems.Add(ds.Tables(0).Rows(y).Item(ds.Tables(0).Columns(x).Caption))
                        End If
                    Next
                    Exit For
                Next


            Case "Single Line Vertical"


                lv.Columns.Add("Property Name")
                lv.Columns.Add("Property Value")

                Dim li As ListViewItem = Nothing

                For x As Integer = 0 To ds.Tables(0).Columns.Count - 1
                    li = lv.Items.Add(ds.Tables(0).Columns(x).Caption)

li.SubItems.Add(ds.Tables(0).Rows(0).Item(ds.Tables(0).Columns(x)))
                Next

        End Select

    End Sub
```

Making the Listview using a DataSet work

To make this code work, we piece together three routines:

Module1.Open_ADO_Recordset_Using_MSPersist("C:\SchemaProducts.xml")
Module1.Create_DataSet_using_ADO_Recordset("Multi Line Horizontal")

Now, depending on what view we want to create:

Orientation:

Multi Line Horizontal

Module1.do_DataSet_code_for_ListView(ListView1, "Multi Line Horizontal")

Multi Line Vertical

Module1.do_DataSet_code_for_ListView(ListView1, "Multi Line Vertical")

Single Line Horizontal

Module1.do_DataSet_code_for_ListView(ListView1, "Single Line Horizontal")

Single Line Vertical

Module1.do_DataSet_code_for_ListView(ListView1, "Single Line Vertical")

Working with the Listview using a DataTable

```vb
Public Sub do_DataTable_code_for_ListView(ByVal lv As ListView, ByVal
Orientation As String)


    lv.Items.Clear()
    lv.Columns.Clear()


    Select Case Orientation


        Case "Multi Line Horizontal"

            For x As Integer = 0 To dt.Columns.Count - 1
                lv.Columns.Add(dt.Columns(x).Caption)
            Next

            Dim li As ListViewItem = Nothing

            For y As Integer = 0 To dt.Rows.Count - 1
                For x As Integer = 0 To dt.Columns.Count - 1
                    If (x = 0) Then
                        li = lv.Items.Add(dt.Rows(y).Item(dt.Columns(x)))
                    Else
                        li.SubItems.Add(dt.Rows(y).Item(dt.Columns(x)))
```

```vbnet
            End If
        Next
    Next


Case "Multi Line Vertical"


    lv.Columns.Add("Property Name")
    For y As Integer = 0 To dt.Rows.Count - 1
        lv.Columns.Add("Row" & y)
    Next

    Dim li As ListViewItem = Nothing

    For x As Integer = 0 To dt.Columns.Count - 1
        li = lv.Items.Add(dt.Columns(x).Caption)
        For y As Integer = 0 To dt.Rows.Count - 1
            li.SubItems.Add(dt.Rows(y).Item(dt.Columns(x).Caption))
        Next
    Next

Case "Single Line Horizontal"


    For x As Integer = 0 To dt.Columns.Count - 1
        lv.Columns.Add(dt.Columns(x).Caption)
    Next

    Dim li As ListViewItem = Nothing

    For y As Integer = 0 To dt.Rows.Count - 1
        For x As Integer = 0 To dt.Columns.Count - 1
            If (x = 0) Then
                li = lv.Items.Add(dt.Rows(y).Item(dt.Columns(x).Caption))
            Else
                li.SubItems.Add(dt.Rows(y).Item(dt.Columns(x).Caption))
            End If
        Next
        Exit For
```

```vb
            Next


        Case "Single Line Vertical"


            lv.Columns.Add("Property Name")
            lv.Columns.Add("Property Value")

            Dim li As ListViewItem = Nothing

            For x As Integer = 0 To dt.Columns.Count - 1
                li = lv.Items.Add(dt.Columns(x).Caption)
                li.SubItems.Add(dt.Rows(0).Item(dt.Columns(x)))
            Next

    End Select

End Sub
```

Making the Listview using a DataTable work

Same routine as the DataSet. Just some name changes:

Module1.Open_ADO_Recordset_Using_MSPersist("C:\SchemaProducts.xml")
Module1.Create_DataTable_using_ADO_Recordset("Multi Line Horizontal")

Now, depending on what view we want to create:

Orientation:

Multi Line Horizontal

Module1.do_DataTable_code_for_ListView(ListView1, "Multi Line Horizontal")

Multi Line Vertical

Module1.do_DataTable_code_for_ListView(ListView1, "Multi Line Vertical")

Single Line Horizontal

Module1.do_DataTable_code_for_ListView(ListView1, "Single Line Horizontal")

Single Line Vertical

Module1.do_DataTable_code_for_ListView(ListView1, "Single Line Vertical")

Working with the Listview using a DataView

```vbnet
Public Sub do_DataView_code_for_ListView(ByVal lv As ListView, ByVal
Orientation As String)


    lv.Items.Clear()
    lv.Columns.Clear()


    Select Case Orientation


      Case "Multi Line Horizontal"

        For x As Integer = 0 To dv.Table.Columns.Count - 1
          lv.Columns.Add(dv.Table.Columns(x).Caption)
        Next

        Dim li As ListViewItem = Nothing

        For y As Integer = 0 To dv.Table.Rows.Count - 1
          For x As Integer = 0 To dv.Table.Columns.Count - 1
            If (x = 0) Then
              li = lv.Items.Add(dv.Table.Rows(y).Item(dv.Table.Columns(x)))
            Else
```

```vbnet
                    li.SubItems.Add(dv.Table.Rows(y).Item(dv.Table.Columns(x)))
                End If
            Next
        Next


    Case "Multi Line Vertical"


        lv.Columns.Add("Property Name")
        For y As Integer = 0 To dv.Table.Rows.Count - 1
          lv.Columns.Add("Row" & y)
        Next

        Dim li As ListViewItem = Nothing

        For x As Integer = 0 To dv.Table.Columns.Count - 1
          li = lv.Items.Add(dv.Table.Columns(x).Caption)
          For y As Integer = 0 To dv.Table.Rows.Count - 1

li.SubItems.Add(dv.Table.Rows(y).Item(dv.Table.Columns(x).Caption))
          Next
        Next

      Case "Single Line Horizontal"


        For x As Integer = 0 To dv.Table.Columns.Count - 1
          lv.Columns.Add(dv.Table.Columns(x).Caption)
        Next

        Dim li As ListViewItem = Nothing

        For y As Integer = 0 To dv.Table.Rows.Count - 1
          For x As Integer = 0 To dv.Table.Columns.Count - 1
            If (x = 0) Then
              li                                                        =
lv.Items.Add(dv.Table.Rows(y).Item(dv.Table.Columns(x).Caption))
            Else
```

```
li.SubItems.Add(dv.Table.Rows(y).Item(dv.Table.Columns(x).Caption))
                End If
            Next
            Exit For
        Next


    Case "Single Line Vertical"


        lv.Columns.Add("Property Name")
        lv.Columns.Add("Property Value")

        Dim li As ListViewItem = Nothing

        For x As Integer = 0 To dv.Table.Columns.Count - 1
            li = lv.Items.Add(dv.Table.Columns(x).Caption)
            li.SubItems.Add(dv.Table.Rows(0).Item(dv.Table.Columns(x)))
        Next

    End Select

    End Sub
```

Making the Listview using a DataView work

Here's the routine:

Module1.Open_ADO_Recordset_Using_MSPersist("C:\SchemaProducts.xml")
Module1.Create_DataView_using_ADO_Recordset("Multi Line Horizontal")

Now, depending on what view we want to create:

Orientation:

Multi Line Horizontal

Module1.do_DataView_code_for_ListView(ListView1, "Multi Line Horizontal")

Multi Line Vertical

Module1.do_DataView_code_for_ListView(ListView1, "Multi Line Vertical")

Single Line Horizontal

Module1.do_DataView_code_for_ListView(ListView1, "Single Line Horizontal")

Single Line Vertical

Module1.do_DataView_code_for_ListView(ListView1, "Single Line Vertical")

Working with the MSFlexgrid using a Dataset

Chapter Subtitle

```
Public    Sub    do_DataSet_code_for_MSFlexGrid(ByVal    fg    As
AxMSFlexGridLib.AxMSFlexGrid, ByVal Orientation As String)


    fg.Clear()



    Select Case Orientation


        Case "Multi Line Horizontal"


            fg.Cols = ds.Tables(0).Columns.Count + 1
            fg.Rows = ds.Tables(0).Rows.Count + 1
            For x As Integer = 0 To ds.Tables(0).Columns.Count - 1
                fg.set_TextMatrix(0, x + 1, ds.Tables(0).Columns(x).Caption)
            Next

            For y As Integer = 0 To ds.Tables(0).Rows.Count - 1
```

```vb
            For x As Integer = 0 To ds.Tables(0).Columns.Count - 1
                fg.set_TextMatrix(y          +          1,          x          +          1,
ds.Tables(0).Rows(y).Item(ds.Tables(0).Columns(x).Caption))
            Next
        Next


    Case "Multi Line Vertical"

        fg.Rows = ds.Tables(0).Columns.Count + 1
        fg.Cols = ds.Tables(0).Rows.Count + 1
        For x As Integer = 0 To ds.Tables(0).Columns.Count - 1
            fg.set_TextMatrix(x + 1, 0, ds.Tables(0).Columns(x).Caption)
        Next

        For y As Integer = 0 To ds.Tables(0).Rows.Count - 1
            For x As Integer = 0 To ds.Tables(0).Columns.Count - 1
                fg.set_TextMatrix(x          +          1,          y          +          1,
ds.Tables(0).Rows(y).Item(ds.Tables(0).Columns(x).Caption))
            Next
        Next


    Case "Single Line Horizontal"


        fg.Cols = ds.Tables(0).Columns.Count + 1
        fg.Rows = 2
        For x As Integer = 0 To ds.Tables(0).Columns.Count - 1
            fg.set_TextMatrix(0, x + 1, ds.Tables(0).Columns(x).Caption)
        Next

        For y As Integer = 0 To ds.Tables(0).Rows.Count - 1
            For x As Integer = 0 To ds.Tables(0).Columns.Count - 1
                fg.set_TextMatrix(y          +          1,          x          +          1,
ds.Tables(0).Rows(y).Item(ds.Tables(0).Columns(x).Caption))
            Next
            Exit For
        Next
```

```vb
        Case "Single Line Vertical"

            fg.Rows = ds.Tables(0).Columns.Count + 1
            fg.Cols = 2
            For x As Integer = 0 To ds.Tables(0).Columns.Count - 1
                fg.set_TextMatrix(x + 1, 0, ds.Tables(0).Columns(x).Caption)
            Next

            For y As Integer = 0 To ds.Tables(0).Rows.Count - 1
                For x As Integer = 0 To ds.Tables(0).Columns.Count - 1
                    fg.set_TextMatrix(x        +        1,        y        +        1,
ds.Tables(0).Rows(y).Item(ds.Tables(0).Columns(x).Caption))
                Next
                Exit For
            Next



        End Select

    End Sub
```

Making the MSFlexgrid using a DataSet work

Module1.Open_ADO_Recordset_Using_MSPersist("C:\SchemaProducts.xml")
Module1.Create_DataSet_using_ADO_Recordset("Multi Line Horizontal")

Now, depending on what view we want to create:

Orientation:

Multi Line Horizontal

Module1.do_DataSet_code_for_MSFlexGrid (AxMSFlexGrid1
, "Multi Line Horizontal")

Multi Line Vertical

Module1.do_DataSet_code_for_MSFlexGrid(AxMSFlexGrid1
, "Multi Line Vertical")

Single Line Horizontal

Module1.do_DataSet_code_for_MSFlexGrid(AxMSFlexGrid1
, "Single Line Horizontal")

Single Line Vertical

Module1.do_DataSet_code_for_MSFlexGrid(`AxMSFlexGrid1`
, "Single Line Vertical")

Working with the MSFlexgrid using a DataTable

Chapter Subtitle

```
Public      Sub      do_DataTable_code_for_MSFlexGrid(ByVal      fg      As
AxMSFlexGridLib.AxMSFlexGrid, ByVal Orientation As String)


    fg.Clear()



    Select Case Orientation


        Case "Multi Line Horizontal"



            fg.Cols = dt.Columns.Count + 1
            fg.Rows = dt.Rows.Count + 1
            For x As Integer = 0 To dt.Columns.Count - 1
                fg.set_TextMatrix(0, x + 1, dt.Columns(x).Caption)
            Next

            For y As Integer = 0 To dt.Rows.Count - 1
```

```
                    For x As Integer = 0 To dt.Columns.Count - 1
                        fg.set_TextMatrix(y          +          1,          x          +          1,
dt.Rows(y).Item(dt.Columns(x).Caption))
                    Next
                Next



            Case "Multi Line Vertical"

                fg.Rows = dt.Columns.Count + 1
                fg.Cols = dt.Rows.Count + 1
                For x As Integer = 0 To dt.Columns.Count - 1
                    fg.set_TextMatrix(x + 1, 0, dt.Columns(x).Caption)
                Next

                For y As Integer = 0 To dt.Rows.Count - 1
                    For x As Integer = 0 To dt.Columns.Count - 1
                        fg.set_TextMatrix(x          +          1,          y          +          1,
dt.Rows(y).Item(dt.Columns(x).Caption))
                    Next
                Next



            Case "Single Line Horizontal"


                fg.Cols = dt.Columns.Count + 1
                fg.Rows = 2
                For x As Integer = 0 To dt.Columns.Count - 1
                    fg.set_TextMatrix(0, x + 1, dt.Columns(x).Caption)
                Next

                For y As Integer = 0 To dt.Rows.Count - 1
                    For x As Integer = 0 To dt.Columns.Count - 1
                        fg.set_TextMatrix(y          +          1,          x          +          1,
dt.Rows(y).Item(dt.Columns(x).Caption))
                    Next
                    Exit For
                Next
```

```
Case "Single Line Vertical"

    fg.Rows = dt.Columns.Count + 1
    fg.Cols = 2
    For x As Integer = 0 To dt.Columns.Count - 1
        fg.set_TextMatrix(x + 1, 0, dt.Columns(x).Caption)
    Next

    For y As Integer = 0 To dt.Rows.Count - 1
        For x As Integer = 0 To dt.Columns.Count - 1
            fg.set_TextMatrix(x      +      1,      y      +      1,
dt.Rows(y).Item(dt.Columns(x).Caption))
        Next
        Exit For
    Next


    End Select

    End Sub
```

Making the MSFlexgrid using a DataTable work

Routines to make the magic happen:

Module1.Open_ADO_Recordset_Using_MSPersist("C:\SchemaProducts.xml")
Module1.Create_DataTable_using_ADO_Recordset("Multi Line Horizontal")

Now, depending on what view we want to create:

Orientation:

Multi Line Horizontal

Module1.do_DataTable_code_for_MSFlexGrid (AxMSFlexGrid1
, "Multi Line Horizontal")

Multi Line Vertical

Module1.do_DataTable_code_for_MSFlexGrid(AxMSFlexGrid1
, "Multi Line Vertical")

Single Line Horizontal

Module1.do_DataTable_code_for_MSFlexGrid(AxMSFlexGrid1
, "Single Line Horizontal")

Single Line Vertical

Module1.do_DataTable_code_for_MSFlexGrid(AxMSFlexGrid1
, "Single Line Vertical")

Working with the MSFlexGrid using a DataView

```
Public      Sub     do_DataView_code_for_MSFlexGrid(ByVal      fg     As
AxMSFlexGridLib.AxMSFlexGrid, ByVal Orientation As String)


    fg.Clear()


    Select Case Orientation


        Case "Multi Line Horizontal"


            fg.Cols = dv.Table.Columns.Count + 1
            fg.Rows = dv.Table.Rows.Count + 1
            For x As Integer = 0 To dv.Table.Columns.Count - 1
                fg.set_TextMatrix(0, x + 1, dv.Table.Columns(x).Caption)
```

```vbnet
            Next

        For y As Integer = 0 To dv.Table.Rows.Count - 1
            For x As Integer = 0 To dv.Table.Columns.Count - 1
                fg.set_TextMatrix(y + 1, x + 1, dv.Table.Rows(y).Item(dv.Table.Columns(x).Caption))
            Next
        Next


    Case "Multi Line Vertical"

        fg.Rows = dv.Table.Columns.Count + 1
        fg.Cols = dv.Table.Rows.Count + 1
        For x As Integer = 0 To dv.Table.Columns.Count - 1
            fg.set_TextMatrix(x + 1, 0, dv.Table.Columns(x).Caption)
        Next

        For y As Integer = 0 To dv.Table.Rows.Count - 1
            For x As Integer = 0 To dv.Table.Columns.Count - 1
                fg.set_TextMatrix(x + 1, y + 1, dv.Table.Rows(y).Item(dv.Table.Columns(x).Caption))
            Next
        Next


    Case "Single Line Horizontal"


        fg.Cols = dv.Table.Columns.Count + 1
        fg.Rows = 2
        For x As Integer = 0 To dv.Table.Columns.Count - 1
            fg.set_TextMatrix(0, x + 1, dv.Table.Columns(x).Caption)
        Next

        For y As Integer = 0 To dv.Table.Rows.Count - 1
            For x As Integer = 0 To dv.Table.Columns.Count - 1
                fg.set_TextMatrix(y + 1, x + 1, dv.Table.Rows(y).Item(dv.Table.Columns(x).Caption))
            Next
```

```
            Exit For
        Next


    Case "Single Line Vertical"

        fg.Rows = dv.Table.Columns.Count + 1
        fg.Cols = 2
        For x As Integer = 0 To dv.Table.Columns.Count - 1
            fg.set_TextMatrix(x + 1, 0, dv.Table.Columns(x).Caption)
        Next

        For y As Integer = 0 To dv.Table.Rows.Count - 1
            For x As Integer = 0 To dv.Table.Columns.Count - 1
                fg.set_TextMatrix(x       +       1,       y       +       1,
dv.Table.Rows(y).Item(dv.Table.Columns(x).Caption))
            Next
            Exit For
        Next



    End Select

    End Sub
```

Making the MSFlexgrid using a DataView work

The Routines:

Module1.Open_ADO_Recordset_Using_MSPersist("C:\SchemaProducts.xml")
Module1.Create_DataView_using_ADO_Recordset("Multi Line Horizontal")

Now, depending on what view we want to create:

Orientation:

Multi Line Horizontal

Module1.do_DataView_code_for_MSFlexGrid (AxMSFlexGrid1
, "Multi Line Horizontal")

Multi Line Vertical

Module1.do_DataView_code_for_MSFlexGrid(AxMSFlexGrid1
, "Multi Line Vertical")

Single Line Horizontal

Module1.do_DataView_code_for_MSFlexGrid(AxMSFlexGrid1
, "Single Line Horizontal")

Single Line Vertical

Module1.do_DataView_code_for_MSFlexGrid(AxMSFlexGrid1
, "Single Line Vertical")

Working with the Spreadsheet using a DataSet

Chapter Subtitle

```vb
Public Sub do_DataSet_code_for_Spreadsheet(ByVal sp1 As AxMicrosoft.Office.Interop.Owc11.AxSpreadsheet, ByVal Orientation As String)


        sp1.ActiveSheet.Cells.Clear()



        Select Case Orientation


            Case "Multi Line Horizontal"


                For x As Integer = 0 To ds.Tables(0).Columns.Count - 1
                    sp1.ActiveSheet.Cells(1, x + 1) = ds.Tables(0).Columns(x).Caption
                Next

                For y As Integer = 0 To ds.Tables(0).Rows.Count - 1
                    For x As Integer = 0 To ds.Tables(0).Columns.Count - 1
                        sp1.ActiveSheet.Cells(y + 2, x + 1) = ds.Tables(0).Rows(y).Item(ds.Tables(0).Columns(x).Caption)
```

```
                Next
            Next


        Case "Multi Line Vertical"

            For x As Integer = 0 To ds.Tables(0).Columns.Count - 1
                sp1.ActiveSheet.Cells(x + 1, 1) = ds.Tables(0).Columns(x).Caption
            Next

            For y As Integer = 0 To ds.Tables(0).Rows.Count - 1
                For x As Integer = 0 To ds.Tables(0).Columns.Count - 1
                    sp1.ActiveSheet.Cells(x     +     1,     y     +     2)     =
ds.Tables(0).Rows(y).Item(ds.Tables(0).Columns(x).Caption)
                Next
            Next


        Case "Single Line Horizontal"


            For x As Integer = 0 To ds.Tables(0).Columns.Count - 1
                sp1.ActiveSheet.Cells(1, x + 1) = ds.Tables(0).Columns(x).Caption
            Next

            For y As Integer = 0 To ds.Tables(0).Rows.Count - 1
                For x As Integer = 0 To ds.Tables(0).Columns.Count - 1
                    sp1.ActiveSheet.Cells(y     +     2,     x     +     1)     =
ds.Tables(0).Rows(y).Item(ds.Tables(0).Columns(x).Caption)
                Next
                Exit For
            Next


        Case "Single Line Vertical"


            For x As Integer = 0 To ds.Tables(0).Columns.Count - 1
                sp1.ActiveSheet.Cells(x + 1, 1) = ds.Tables(0).Columns(x).Caption
            Next
```

```vb
        For y As Integer = 0 To ds.Tables(0).Rows.Count - 1
            For x As Integer = 0 To ds.Tables(0).Columns.Count - 1
                sp1.ActiveSheet.Cells(x      +      1,      y      +      2)      =
ds.Tables(0).Rows(y).Item(ds.Tables(0).Columns(x).Caption)
            Next
            Exit For
        Next


    End Select

End Sub
```

Making the Spreadsheet using a DataSet work

This will get it done:

Module1.Open_ADO_Recordset_Using_MSPersist("C:\SchemaProducts.xml")
Module1.Create_DataSet_using_ADO_Recordset("Multi Line Horizontal")

Now, depending on what view we want to create:

Orientation:

Multi Line Horizontal

Module1.do_DataSet_code_for_Spreadsheet (AxSpreadsheet1

, "Multi Line Horizontal")

Multi Line Vertical

Module1.do_DataSet_code_for_Spreadsheet(AxSpreadsheet1

, "Multi Line Vertical")

Single Line Horizontal

Module1.do_DataSet_code_for_Spreadsheet(AxSpreadsheet1
, "Single Line Horizontal")

Single Line Vertical

Module1.do_DataSet_code_for_Spreadsheet(AxSpreadsheet1
, "Single Line Vertical")

Working with the Spreadsheet using a DataTable

Chapter Subtitle

```
Public    Sub    do_DataTable_code_for_Spreadsheet(ByVal    sp1    As
AxMicrosoft.Office.Interop.Owc11.AxSpreadsheet, ByVal Orientation As String)


    sp1.ActiveSheet.Cells.Clear()



    Select Case Orientation


        Case "Multi Line Horizontal"


            For x As Integer = 0 To dt.Columns.Count - 1
              sp1.ActiveSheet.Cells(1, x + 1) = dt.Columns(x).Caption
            Next

            For y As Integer = 0 To dt.Rows.Count - 1
              For x As Integer = 0 To dt.Columns.Count - 1
                sp1.ActiveSheet.Cells(y    +    2,    x    +    1)    =
dt.Rows(y).Item(dt.Columns(x).Caption)
```

```
                Next
            Next


        Case "Multi Line Vertical"

            For x As Integer = 0 To dt.Columns.Count - 1
                sp1.ActiveSheet.Cells(x + 1, 1) = dt.Columns(x).Caption
            Next

            For y As Integer = 0 To dt.Rows.Count - 1
                For x As Integer = 0 To dt.Columns.Count - 1
                    sp1.ActiveSheet.Cells(x     +     1,    y    +    2)    =
dt.Rows(y).Item(dt.Columns(x).Caption)
                Next
            Next


        Case "Single Line Horizontal"


            For x As Integer = 0 To dt.Columns.Count - 1
                sp1.ActiveSheet.Cells(1, x + 1) = dt.Columns(x).Caption
            Next

            For y As Integer = 0 To dt.Rows.Count - 1
                For x As Integer = 0 To dt.Columns.Count - 1
                    sp1.ActiveSheet.Cells(y     +     2,    x    +    1)    =
dt.Rows(y).Item(dt.Columns(x).Caption)
                Next
                Exit For
            Next


        Case "Single Line Vertical"


            For x As Integer = 0 To dt.Columns.Count - 1
                sp1.ActiveSheet.Cells(x + 1, 1) = dt.Columns(x).Caption
            Next
```

```vbnet
            For y As Integer = 0 To dt.Rows.Count - 1
                For x As Integer = 0 To dt.Columns.Count - 1
                    sp1.ActiveSheet.Cells(x     +     1,     y     +     2)     =
dt.Rows(y).Item(dt.Columns(x).Caption)
                Next
                Exit For
            Next


        End Select

    End Sub
```

Making the Spreadsheet using a DataTable work

Another set of routines:

Module1.Open_ADO_Recordset_Using_MSPersist("C:\SchemaProducts.xml")
Module1.Create_DataTable_using_ADO_Recordset("Multi Line Horizontal")

Now, depending on what view we want to create:

Orientation:

Multi Line Horizontal

Module1.do_DataTable_code_for_Spreadsheet (AxSpreadsheet1

, "Multi Line Horizontal")

Multi Line Vertical

Module1.do_DataTable_code_for_Spreadsheet(AxSpreadsheet1

, "Multi Line Vertical")

Single Line Horizontal

Module1.do_DataTable_code_for_Spreadsheet(AxSpreadsheet1
, "Single Line Horizontal")

Single Line Vertical

Module1.do_DataTable_code_for_Spreadsheet(AxSpreadsheet1
, "Single Line Vertical")

Working with the Spreadsheet using a DataView

```vb
Public     Sub     do_DataView_code_for_Spreadsheet(ByVal     sp1     As
AxMicrosoft.Office.Interop.Owc11.AxSpreadsheet, ByVal Orientation As String)


    sp1.ActiveSheet.Cells.Clear()


    Select Case Orientation


        Case "Multi Line Horizontal"


            For x As Integer = 0 To dv.Table.Columns.Count - 1
                sp1.ActiveSheet.Cells(1, x + 1) = dv.table.Columns(x).Caption
            Next

            For y As Integer = 0 To dv.Table.Rows.Count - 1
                For x As Integer = 0 To dv.Table.Columns.Count - 1
                    sp1.ActiveSheet.Cells(y     +     2,     x     +     1)     =
dv.table.Rows(y).Item(dv.table.Columns(x).Caption)
                Next
            Next
```

```
        Case "Multi Line Vertical"

            For x As Integer = 0 To dv.Table.Columns.Count - 1
                sp1.ActiveSheet.Cells(x + 1, 1) = dv.table.Columns(x).Caption
            Next

            For y As Integer = 0 To dv.Table.Rows.Count - 1
                For x As Integer = 0 To dv.Table.Columns.Count - 1
                    sp1.ActiveSheet.Cells(x    +    1,    y    +    2)    =
dv.table.Rows(y).Item(dv.table.Columns(x).Caption)
                Next
            Next


        Case "Single Line Horizontal"

            For x As Integer = 0 To dv.Table.Columns.Count - 1
                sp1.ActiveSheet.Cells(1, x + 1) = dv.table.Columns(x).Caption
            Next

            For y As Integer = 0 To dv.Table.Rows.Count - 1
                For x As Integer = 0 To dv.Table.Columns.Count - 1
                    sp1.ActiveSheet.Cells(y    +    2,    x    +    1)    =
dv.Table.Rows(y).Item(dv.Table.Columns(x).Caption)
                Next
                Exit For
            Next


        Case "Single Line Vertical"

            For x As Integer = 0 To dv.Table.Columns.Count - 1
                sp1.ActiveSheet.Cells(x + 1, 1) = dv.table.Columns(x).Caption
            Next

            For y As Integer = 0 To dv.Table.Rows.Count - 1
                For x As Integer = 0 To dv.Table.Columns.Count - 1
```

```
                    sp1.ActiveSheet.Cells(x       +       1,       y       +       2)       =
dv.Table.Rows(y).Item(dv.Table.Columns(x).Caption)
                    Next
                    Exit For
                Next


            End Select

        End Sub


        End Module
```

Making the Spreadsheet using a DataView work

Getting boring, yet? Okay, the routines for the DataView.

Module1.Open_ADO_Recordset_Using_MSPersist("C:\SchemaProducts.xml")
Module1.Create_DataView_using_ADO_Recordset("Multi Line Horizontal")

Now, depending on what view we want to create:

Orientation:

Multi Line Horizontal

Module1.do_DataView_code_for_Spreadsheet (AxSpreadsheet1

, "Multi Line Horizontal")

Multi Line Vertical

Module1.do_DataView_code_for_Spreadsheet(AxSpreadsheet1

, "Multi Line Vertical")

Single Line Horizontal

Module1.do_DataView_code_for_Spreadsheet(AxSpreadsheet1
, "Single Line Horizontal")

Single Line Vertical

Module1.do_DataView_code_for_Spreadsheet(AxSpreadsheet1
, "Single Line Vertical")

To summarize

This book is what I call a core book. That means that around 6 variations of this book is possible with only the recordset routine being changed out.

I'm telling you this because it is important for you to know in advance that unless you want to see the same routines in each book, I'm being honest here. Purchase the e-book or read it for free, Get the code that makes the book different.

Good luck and happy coding!